Ninja Blender
Cookbook

Ninja Blender
Cookbook

Fast, Healthy Blender Recipes for Soups, Sauces,

Smoothies, Dips, and More

DYLANNAPRESS

Contents

1

WHETHER YOU'RE NEW to the world of high-speed blenders or have been using a Ninja Blender for years, the *Ninja Blender Cookbook: Fast Healthy Blender Recipes for Soups, Sauces, Smoothies, Dips, and More* is going to help you make amazingly healthy and delicious soups, dips, sauces, smoothies, desserts, and more.

Many people are excited when they first purchase a Ninja Blender but aren't really sure what to do with it besides make smoothies. While the Ninja Blender is great for making smoothies it has the potential to be used for so much more.

This book contains a plethora of recipes that can all be made quickly and easily right in your Ninja Blender. So what are you waiting for?

Happy blending!

Ninja Blender Basics

Ninja blenders are well-loved by both home cooks and professional chefs alike. They are known for their extremely high quality and durability. The Ninja Blender offers a fabulous high-speed blending experience for a very economical price. Its main distinguishing feature is dual-stage blending, with a second detachable blade up higher in the blender. This powerful features helps the Ninja Blender t power through where other blenders get stuck.

A Ninja Blender is more than just a blender. In fact, it can take the place of a whole host of appliances including a food processor, juicer, meat grinder, and ice cream maker. You can use it for so many purposes including blending, chopping, pureeing, and grinding to make a whole host of recipes from dips and spreads to nut butters and milks to soups, smoothies, sorbets, and much more.

With your Ninja Blender and the recipes in this book you will be inspired to create healthy and delicious meals easier than you ever thought possible.

Ninja Blender Model Comparisons

It can be hard to choose among all of the Ninja models currently available. Here is a brief overview of the various models and features and the differences between them.

Ninja Ultima Series
The Ultima series features a 1500 watt, 2.5 horsepower motor to provide for total crushing power. The blender is not only able to break down ice, but whole fruits and vegetables as well. Its high-speed cyclonic technology is great for pureeing foods and making them smooth and creamy. It comes equipped with

10 speeds and pulse capability.
Ninja Ultima Models

Model	BL800	BL810	BL820	BL830
Accessories	None	2 single serve cups & lids Single serve blade assembly	2 single serve cups & lids Single serve blade assembly Slicing disc Grating disc Feed chute lid Drizzle hold lid 64 ounce food processing bowl Disc adapter Food pusher Dough blade	3 single serve cups & lids Single serve blade assembly
Speeds	Preset dial: Low Medium, High	10 speed variable dial	10 speed variable dial	10 speed variable dial
Power	1500W/ 2.5 peak horsepower	1500W/ 2.5 peak horsepower	1500W/ 3 peak horsepower	1500W/ 2.5 peak horsepower

Ninja Professional Blender

The Ninja Professional blender features a 1000 watt motor and 6 blade technology. It is able to crush ice as well as whole fruits and vegetables. It comes with a 72 ounce pitcher and a locking lid. The Professional blender has three speeds as well as a pulse feature.

Ninja Kitchen System Pulse

The Ninja Pulse has a 550 watt motor and is smaller in size than either the Ultima or the Professional. it has a single button and one speed and comes complete with a 4-ounce pitcher, as well as a separate 40-ounce food processing bowl with blade, a blade for dough mixing, a shredding disc with adapter and two single serve, 16-ounce cups with lids.

Which One Should You Buy?

Which one you should buy depends on what you plan on using it for as well your budget. All three blenders are powerful and perform well across a whole range of tasks.
The recipes in this book have been tested using the Ninja Ultima.

High-Speed Blenders v. Juicers

You might be wondering what the difference is between a high-speed blender, such as a Vitamix, and a juicer. The main difference is that a juicer separates the juice from the fiber while a blender blends all of the ingredients together. This means that fruits and vegetables blended in a blender retain the pulp and fiber.

A blender contains blades that are normally placed in the base of the unit. These blades cut, pulverize, and blend whatever foods you put into the blender. It does not separate out the juice from the pulp, seeds, and skin as a juicer does. Therefore, a blender will producer thicker drinks and smoothies than a juicer does. Blenders contain powerful motors that are also capable of crushing ice.

Which type of appliance you choose depends on what you intend to use it for. Blenders are perfect for making things like smoothies, soups, and sauces. A juicer is great for making your own juices such as orange, carrot, or tomato juice.

Tips for Using Your Ninja Blender

To get the most from your Ninja Blender, there are a few simple tips to follow.

Layering properly is key. The order in which you place your ingredients into the blender is important so don't just throw them in there haphazardly. Start with liquids first, followed by light or small ingredients, and top with the largest and heaviest ingredients.

Cut ingredients before adding. The best size for most fruits and vegetables is about 1-inch cubes.

Add ice cubes last. Use whole cubes, not crushed, and put them on top of other ingredients.

Use enough liquid. If you find that your blender is getting clogged and things are not blending properly, adding a little water or other liquid can help lift the ingredients off the blades and ensure an even blend.

Start off slow. For most recipes, start at a slow speed for a few seconds and then turn it to high. This allows the blades to grab on to the ingredients easier.

Use it as a food processor. The Ninja Blender does a great job chopping vegetables as well as pureeing them.

Don't worry about the noise. When grinding hard ingredients, such as nuts, the machine is going to sound loud, this is normal. Don't worry, your are not ruining the engine.

Use hot water. If you're making soup or a hot sauce, use the hottest tap water. This will make your soups and sauces hotter and more flavorful.

Let it clean itself. Rinse it out right after using it. Fill halfway with water, add a drop or two of detergent and blend for a minute or so. Pour out soapy water and rinse with fresh water.

2

Nuts about Nuts

....

Nut milks, nut butters, nut flours—so many ways to make use of nuts in a Ninja Blender. Making your own will save you money, plus the flavor variations are virtually endless.

ALMOND MILK

··

Making your own almond milk is simple and it taste delicious. Since your making your own you have complete control over how much sweetener, if any, to add. Remember, the nuts will need to be soaked for at least 4-6 hours before blending, so plan ahead by soaking them in water overnight. Almond milk is great for drinking, in your coffee, on your cereal, and for baking.

Servings: 5 cups

··

1 1/2 cups raw almonds, blanched (can also use regular almonds)

4 cups water

Optional additions:

1 teaspoon vanilla extract

1/2 teaspoon cinnamon

1 tablespoon honey or other sweetener

Pinch of sea salt

··

1.   Place almonds in a large bowl and cover with water. Soak for a minimum of 4 hours. The longer the better.

2.   Strain off water and place almonds into your blender. Add 2 cups of water and blend for 2-3 minutes until a thick paste is formed.

3.   Add in remaining water and any of the optional ingredients. Blend for another 2-3 minutes until milk is smooth and frothy.

4.   Now it is time to strain the almond milk. Place a metal strainer over a large bowl. Spread a couple of layers of cheesecloth over the strainer. Slowly pour the almond milk through the strainer. Squeeze cheesecloth to remove excess milk.

5.   Pour milk into glass container with cover and store in refrigerator for 3-4 days.

Tip: If you are going to be making nut milks regularly, then you may want to invest in a nut milk bag. These bags are much finer than cheesecloth and will give you the smoothest quality milk. They are available online and run under $10.

CASHEW MILK

....

Cashew milk is very creamy and delicious and unlike other nut milks, no straining is required. Cashew milk is very nutritious, is an excellent source of protein, and is full of heart healthy unsaturated fats. Use it in coffee, for Chai tea, with your morning granola, or just by itself, cold in a glass.

Servings: 5 cups

....

1 1/2 cups raw cashews

4 cups water

Optional additions

1 1/2 teaspoons vanilla extract

1 tablespoon honey or other sweetener

Pinch of salt

1/2 teaspoon cinnamon

....

1.   Place cashews in a bowl. Cover with water and soak for a minimum of 4 hours or overnight. Drain.

2.   Add cashews to blender and pour in 2 cups of water. Blend, starting on low, and slowly increasing speed, for 2 minutes.

3.   Add remaining water, any optional ingredients, and blend for another 2-3 minutes until milk is smooth and frothy.

4.   Store in glass container with lid in refrigerator for 3-4 days.

MAPLE-PECAN MILK

....

This is another great tasting nut milk that is full of nutrients. This flavor combination is a favorite in oatmeal.

Servings: 5 cups

....

1 1/2 cups raw pecans, blanched
4 cups water
1-2 tablespoons pure maple syrup
Pinch of sea salt

....

1.   Place pecans in a large bowl and cover with water. Soak for a minimum of 4 hours.

2.   Strain off water and place pecans into your blender. Add 2 cups of water and blend for 2-3 minutes until a thick paste is formed.

3.   Add in remaining water, maple syrup, and salt. Blend for another 2-3 minutes until milk is smooth and frothy.

4.   Place a metal strainer over a large bowl. Spread a couple of layers of cheesecloth over the strainer. Slowly pour the pecan milk through the strainer. Squeeze cheesecloth to remove excess milk.

5.   Pour milk into glass container with cover and store in refrigerator for 3-4 days.

COCONUT MILK

Coconut milk is very nutritious as it contains lauric acid and medium chain fatty acids which have been shown to be heart healthy and help with weight loss. It can be used in all kinds of recipes including smoothies, baked goods, curries, and as a standalone drink.

Servings: 4 cups

2 cups shredded coconut, unsweetened
3 cups hot water

1.	Add coconut and water to blender. Process on high for 3-4 minutes or until desired consistency is reached.

2.	To strain, place metal colander over large bowl. Line with a couple of layers of cheesecloth. Pour coconut milk through colander.

3.	Store in glass container with cover in refrigerator for 3-4 days. Shake before serving.

PISTACHIO MILK

....

Pistachio milk has a strong, distinctive taste that works well in dessert recipes such as ice cream or puddings. They do not need to be soaked in advance.

Servings: 5 cups

....

1 cup raw pistachio nuts, unsalted

4 cups water

Optional additions:

1 teaspoon vanilla extract

1 tablespoon honey or other sweetener

Pinch of sea salt

....

1.   Place pistachios into your blender. Add 2 cups of water and blend for 1-2minutes until pistachios are pulverized.

2.   Add in remaining water and any of the optional ingredients. Blend for another 2-3 minutes until milk is smooth and frothy.

3.   Place a metal strainer over a large bowl. Spread a couple of layers of cheesecloth over the strainer. Slowly pour the pistachio milk through the strainer. Squeeze cheesecloth to remove excess milk.

4.   Pour milk into glass container with cover and store in refrigerator for 3-4 days.

CHOCOLATE ALMOND MILK

Rich dark chocolate and nutty taste is like a candy bar in a glass.

Servings: 4

1 cup raw almonds, blanched

4 cups water

1/4 cup raw cacao nibs

Pinch of salt

1 tablespoon honey or maple syrup (optional)

1.   Place almonds in a large bowl and cover with water. Soak for a minimum of 4 hours and preferable overnight.

2.   Strain off water and place almonds into your blender. Add 2 cups of water and blend for 2-3 minutes until a thick paste is formed.

3.   Add in remaining water, cacao nibs, salt, and honey or maple syrup. Blend for another 2-3 minutes until milk is smooth and frothy.

4.   Place a metal strainer over a large bowl. Spread a couple of layers of cheesecloth over the strainer. Slowly pour the almond milk through the strainer. Squeeze cheesecloth to remove excess milk.

5.   Pour milk into glass container with cover and store in refrigerator for 3-4 days.

STRAWBERRY COCONUT MILK

This tastes like a strawberry pina colada.

Servings: 4 cups

2 cups shredded coconut, unsweetened

3 cups water

2 cups strawberries, fresh or frozen (thawed), stems removed

1 tablespoon honey

1 teaspoon vanilla extract

1.   Add all ingredients to blender. Process on high for 3-4 minutes or until completely combined

2.   To strain, place metal colander over large bowl. Line with a couple of layers of cheesecloth. Pour coconut milk through colander.

3.   Store in glass container with cover in refrigerator for 3-4 days. Shake before serving.

COCONUT BUTTER

Making your own coconut butter couldn't be simpler and will definitely save you money. Coconut butter has a rich coconut taste and is extremely versatile. It can be used in baking, added to smoothies, or stirred into your morning coffee in place of cream for a rich nutty taste.

Servings: 2 ½ cups

6 cups coconut flakes, unsweetened

1.   Pour coconut flakes into blender. Blend on high for 60 seconds. Push down coconut flakes from side of blender. Process for another minute or until desired consistency is reached.

2.   Coconut butter can be stored at room temperature in an airtight container for several months. If stored in refrigerator butter will turn hard—bring to room temperature to soften.

Tip: People often wonder about the difference between coconut butter and coconut oil. Unlike coconut butter, coconut oil is a liquid at room temperature and does not contain the meat of the coconut. Coconut oil is better for cooking at high temperatures, such as for stir frying.

ALMOND FLOUR

....

Making your own almond flour, or any nut flour really, is simple and economical. Use for all your gluten-free baking products – cookies, cakes, pancakes, even bread.

Servings: 2 cups

....

2 cups raw almonds or blanched almonds

....

1.   Place almonds into your blender. Process on high for 15-20 seconds. Done!
2.   Store in airtight container for up to 4 weeks.

Tip: This can be done with any other type of nut you desire. Try it for pecan flour, hazelnut flour, and walnut flour.

COCONUT FLOUR

....

Making your own coconut flour from shredded coconut couldn't be easier. Coconut flour can be used for all of your gluten-free baking needs and is rich in nutrients.

Servings: 1 cup

....

2 cups shredded coconut

....

1.   Place shredded coconut in blender using dry container. Make sure there is no moisture in it.

2.   Blend on high for 30 seconds. Tamp down sides. Blend for 15 seconds. Tamp down side. Repeat process until all flakes have turned into powder.

3.   Store in airtight container.

PEANUT BUTTER

....

Making your own peanut butter ensures that it doesn't have trans fats or huge amounts of added sugar.

Servings: 1 cup

....

3 cups raw peanuts
½ cup oil – olive oil, sunflower oil, or peanut oil are all acceptable
Pinch of sea salt

....

1.   Put peanuts, oil and salt into blender. Start on low and then bring it up to high speed. Blend for 60 seconds. Check consistency. TBlend for another 30-60 seconds if needed.
2.   Store in airtight container in refrigerator for up to 3-4 weeks.

Tip: Add a little honey (around 1 tablespoon) for a sweeter tasting butter.

ALMOND BUTTER

....

Almond butter is becoming increasingly popular as an alternative to peanut butter. Almond butter is rich in vitamin E, potassium, magnesium, iron, calcium, phosphorus, fiber, and healthy monounsaturated fats. Plus, you can make your own at a fraction of the cost of store bought.

Servings: 1 cup

....

3 cups almonds, raw or roasted
½ cup oil (optional, adding oil will give a creamier butter)

....

1.   Place nuts in blender. Add oil if desired. Turn blender to low and then increase to high. Blend for 1 minute. Check consistency. Blend for additional minute if needed.
2.   Store in airtight container in refrigerator for up to 1 month.

SWEET VANILLA ROASTED CASHEW BUTTER

Roasting the nuts before grinding enriches the flavor. This is a sweet and salty combination.

Servings: 1 cup

3 cups cashews

3 tablespoons honey

1 teaspoon vanilla extract

Pinch of sea salt

½ teaspoon cinnamon

1.   Heat oven to 350 degrees. Spread cashews on baking sheet in single layer (may need more than one pan).

2.   Sprinkle cashews lightly with water. Place in oven and roast for 20 minutes, stirring once or twice during that time.

3.   Remove nuts from oven and allow to cool.

4.   Put cashews, honey, vanilla, salt, and cinnamon into blender. Start on low and then increase speed to high for 1 minute. Check consistency and blend for up to 1 more minute.

5.   Store in airtight container in refrigerator for up to 1 month.

MAPLE PECAN BUTTER

Another delicious flavor combination. Try this on sprouted grain toast.

Servings: 1 cup

3 cups pecans
2 tablespoons pure maple syrup
Pinch of sea salt

1.   Place pecans, maple syrup, and salt in blender. Start on low and then increase speed to high for 1 minute. Check consistency and blend for up to 1 more minute.

2.   Store in airtight container in refrigerator for up to 1 month.

DARK CHOCOLATE HAZELNUT BUTTER

....

This homemade version of Nutella is positively addicting.

Servings: 2 cups

....

2 ½ cups hazelnuts

¼ cup raw cacao nibs or 2 tablespoons cacao powder

3 tablespoons cane sugar or honey

½ teaspoon vanilla extract

Pinch of sea salt

....

1.   Heat oven to 350 degrees F. Spread hazelnuts on baking sheet in single layer and roast in oven for 15 minutes, stirring once.

2.   Remove hazelnuts from and oven place in clean dish towel while they are still hot. Fold towel around hazelnuts and massage with hands so nuts are rubbed against one another. This will cause skins to fall off.

3.   Place hazelnuts in blender, discard skins.

4.   Add cacao, sugar, vanilla, and salt to blender. Start on low and then increase speed to high for 1 minute. TCheck consistency and blend for up to 1 more minute or until consistency is creamy.

5.   Store in airtight container in refrigerator for up to 1 month.

SUNFLOWER SEED BUTTER

This very nutrition seed butter is a great alternative for people with nut allergens.

Servings: 1 ½ cups

2 ½ cups raw sunflower seeds, hulled

2 tablespoons sunflower oil or coconut oil

Pinch of sea salt

1.   Heat oven to 350 degrees F. Spread sunflower seeds in single layer on baking sheet(s). Roast for about 15 minutes or until golden brown, stirring frequently.

2.   Remove from oven and allow to cool.

3.   Put seeds, oil, and salt in blender. Start on low and then increase speed to high for 1 minute. Check consistency and blend for up to 1 more minute or until smooth and creamy.

4.   Store in airtight container in refrigerator for up to 1 month.

MACADAMIA-CASHEW NUT BUTTER

Rich, creamy, delicious, this combination is so good you will want to eat it by the spoonful.

Servings: 2 cups

2 cups macadamia nuts

1 cup cashews

2 tablespoon coconut oil

3-4 tablespoons pure maple syrup

1 teaspoon vanilla extract

Pinch of salt (generous)

1.   Add macadamia nuts and cashews to blender. Process for about a minute. Add coconut oil, maple syrup, vanilla, and salt. Blend for an additional minute or until desired creaminess is reached.

2.   Store in airtight container in refrigerator for up to a month.

3

Blender Burgers

BLACK BEAN BURGERS

....

These high-protein burgers are packed with fiber and low in both calories and fat. Make a double batch to freeze for later.

Servings: 4

....

1 (16 ounce) can black beans, drained and rinsed

1 medium yellow onion, diced

1 carrot, shredded

3 cloves garlic, minced

½ cup corn, fresh or frozen (thawed)

1 egg

½ cup Panko-style bread crumbs

¼ cup fresh cilantro, chopped

1 tablespoon cumin powder

Salt and freshly ground black pepper, to taste

....

1.   Place all ingredients into blender. Pulse on and off, on speed 8, several times. Press ingredients down toward blades. Pulse a few more times.

2.   Remove bean mixture from blender and place in bowl. Form into 4 patties.

3.   Place patties onto lightly greased baking sheet. Bake in preheated 375 degree F oven for 10 minutes. Flip and bake another 10 minutes.

SPICY CHICKEN BURGERS

....

Making your own chicken burgers is very easy with the help of your Ninja Blender.

Servings: 4

....

1 pound boneless, skinless chicken, cut into chunks

1 medium white onion, diced

1 medium red bell pepper, diced

2 cloves garlic

1 tablespoon Dijon mustard

½ cup bread crumbs

¼ cup fresh cilantro

2 tablespoons lime juice

1 tablespoon hot sauce

1 teaspoon chili powder

1 teaspoon cumin

Salt and freshly ground black pepper, to taste

....

1.   Place all ingredients into blender. Pulse on and off, on speed 8, several times. Press ingredients down toward blades. Pulse a few more times.

2.   Remove mixture from blender and form into 4 patties.

3.   Cook patties on grill or frying pan until no longer pink in center, about 4-5 minutes per side.

BLACK BEAN AND BEET BURGERS

Another take on black bean burgers, this time with the antioxidant power of beets.

Servings: 4

1 (16 ounce) can black beans

2 medium beets, cooked, cut into chunks

½ red onion, chopped

½ cup brown rice, cooked

2 cloves garlic, minced

1 teaspoon paprika

1 teaspoon cumin

Salt and freshly ground black pepper, to taste

1.   Preheat oven to 400 degrees F.

2.   Place all ingredients into blender. Pulse on and off, on speed 8, several times. Press ingredients down toward blades. Pulse a few more times.

3.   Remove mixture from blender and place in bowl. Taste and adust seasonings as needed. Form into 4 patties.

4.   Place patties onto lightly greased baking sheet (or use parchment paper). Bake in preheated 400 degree F oven for 15 minutes. Flip and bake another 10 minutes, until burgers are lightly browned and crisp.

LENTIL QUINOA BURGERS

··

These burgers are very nutritious and taste great.

Servings: 4

··

1 cup cooked lentils

1 cup cooked quinoa

½ red onion, diced

2 cloves garlic

1 egg

1/3 cup oats

½ cup bread crumbs, Panko or regular style

2 teaspoon lemon juice

1 teaspoon paprika

½ teaspoon cumin

Salt and freshly ground black pepper, to taste

2 teaspoons olive oil

··

1.   Place all ingredients, except for olive oil, into blender. Pulse on and off, on speed 8, several times. Press ingredients down toward blades. Pulse a few more times.

2.   Remove mixture from blender and form into 4 patties.

3.   Heat olive oil in large skillet over medium high heat. Add patties and cook until lightly browned, about 5 minutes. Flip and cook on other side until lightly browned, another 5 minutes.

WALNUT-RICE BURGERS

....

These burgers can be frozen after cooking and microwaved for a quick and healthy meal.

Servings: 8

....

2 cups brown rice, cooked
1 cup walnuts
2 tablespoons olive oil, divided
½ small yellow onion, diced
2 cloves garlic, minced
1 stalk celery, chopped
1 small carrot, chopped
½ teaspoon cayenne pepper
½ teaspoon dried ginger powder
1 teaspoon dried basil
1 teaspoon dried thyme
¼ cup fresh parsley
¼ cup whole wheat flour
1 egg, beaten
Salt and freshly ground black pepper, to taste

....

1.

1. Heat 1 tablespoon olive oil in large skillet over medium-high heat. Add onion, garlic, celery, and carrots and sauté for 5-6 minutes until vegetables soften.

2. Add rice, walnuts, vegetables, seasonings, parsley, flour, egg, salt, and pepper to blender.

3. Blend on high for about a minute. Press ingredients down toward blades. Pulse a few more times.

4. Remove mixture from blender and form into 8 patties.

5. Heat 1 tablespoon olive oil in large skillet over medium-high heat. Add patties and cook until lightly browned, about 5 minutes. Flip and cook on other side until lightly browned, another 5 minutes.

CURRIED CHICKPEA BURGERS

....

These burgers are delicious when served in a whole-wheat pita and topped with tzatziki sauce.

Servings: 4

....

1 small yellow onion, chopped

2 cloves garlic, chopped

1 carrot, shredded

¼ cup oats

3 eggs, lightly beaten

1 (15.5 ounce) can chickpeas, rinsed and drained

¼ cup Panko breadcrumbs

1 tablespoon lemon juice

2 teaspoons curry powder

Salt and freshly ground black pepper, to taste

1 tablespoon olive oil

....

1.   Add onion, garlic, carrot, and oats to blender. Process on high for 30 seconds. Add remaining ingredients, except for olive oil, and pulse to mix, leaving mixture somewhat chunky. Form into 4 patties.

2.   Heat 1 tablespoon olive oil in large skillet over medium-high heat. Add patties and cook until golden brown, about 5 minutes. Flip and cook on other side until golden brown, another 5 minutes.

3.   Serve in warm pita pocket topped with tzatziki.

CHICKPEA, SESAME, AND CARROT BURGER

Another take on the ever-popular chickpea burgers. Try these on the grill at your next barbecue.

Servings: 6

1 (15.5 ounce) can chickpeas

1 cup shredded carrots, divided

1 small yellow onion, diced

2 tablespoons tahini paste

1 teaspoon cumin

1 egg, lightly beaten

3 tablespoons olive oil, divided

½ cup breadcrumbs

1 teaspoon lemon juice

3 tablespoons sesame seeds

Salt and freshly ground black pepper, to taste

1.   Put chickpeas, ½ cup carrots, onion, tahini, cumin, and egg into blender. Blend on high for about 1 minute until paste-like consistency is reached. Scoop mixture into bowl.

2.   Heat 1 tablespoon olive oil in large skillet over medium-high heat. Add remaining ½ cup of carrots and cook until softened, about 5-6 minutes.

3.   Add cooked carrots, breadcrumbs, lemon juice, sesame seeds, salt, and pepper to bowl with chickpea mixture.

4.   Mix together using hands or wooden spoon.

5.   Form mixture into 6 equal-size patties. Brush each side with olive oil and cook on preheated grill until golden brown, about 5 minutes per side. Alternatively, cook in skillet over medium-high heat.

GINGER-SPICED SALMON BURGERS

....

Salmon is rich in heart-healthy omega-3s.

Servings: 4

....

1 (14.75 ounce) can wild salmon

1 cup cooked brown rice

¼ cup chopped green onion

1 garlic clove, chopped

2 teaspoons fresh ginger, minced

¼ cup cilantro leaves

1 egg, lightly beaten

2 tablespoons whole wheat flour

Salt and freshly ground black pepper, to taste

2 tablespoons olive oil

....

1.   Place all ingredients into blender except for olive oil. Pulse on and off, on speed 8, several times. Press ingredients down toward blades. Pulse a few more times.

2.   Remove mixture from blender and form into 4 patties. Chill in refrigerator for 30-60 minutes.

3.   Heat olive oil in large skillet over medium high heat. Add patties and cook until lightly browned, about 4 minutes. Flip and cook on other side until lightly browned, another 3 minutes.

FALAFEL

Okay, these aren't technically burgers, but they're pretty close. Serve these in pita bread topped with tahini sauce or on a platter with crudités and hummus.

Servings: 6

2 (15.5 ounce) cans chickpeas, rinsed and drained

1 small onion, chopped

2-3 garlic cloves, chopped

½ cup parsley, chopped

1 teaspoon coriander

1 tablespoon cumin

1 teaspoon sea salt

½ teaspoon freshly ground black pepper

2 tablespoons whole wheat flour

1 tablespoon lemon juice

2-3 tablespoons olive oil

1.   Place all ingredients except for olive oil into blender. Pulse on and off until processed but still a little chunky.

2.   Form mixture into golf-ball size balls. Chill in refrigerator for 30-60 minutes.

3.   Heat olive oil in large frying pan over medium-high heat. Add balls in batches, and fry, turning, until all sides are golden brown, about 4-5 minutes. Set on paper-towel lined plate while cooking remaining batches.

4

Super Soups

CREAMY COCONUT-PUMPKIN SOUP

This creamy soup is perfect on a brisk autumn day.

Servings: 4

2 cups chicken broth

½ cup coconut milk, unsweetened

1 (15 ounce) can pumpkin puree

½ onion, chopped

1 clove garlic, minced

1/2 teaspoon cayenne pepper

½ cup plain Greek yogurt

1 teaspoon honey

Salt and freshly ground black pepper, to taste

1.   Place all ingredients into blender. Turn on low and slowly increase speed to high. Blend for 5-6 minutes until creamy.

2.   Serve topped with croutons.

ROASTED BUTTERNUT SQUASH SOUP

....

Roasting the squash before pureeing gives this soup a rich taste.

Servings: 6

....

2 cups winter squash, cubed (butternut, acorn, Hubbard)

1/2 cup carrots, diced

½ cup onion, diced

½ cup celery diced

1 tablespoon olive oil

1 teaspoon cinnamon

4 cups chicken broth

½ teaspoon coriander

½ cup light cream (optional)

Salt and freshly ground black pepper, to taste

....

1.   Heat oven to 375 degrees F. Arrange winter squash, carrots, onion, and celery on baking sheet. Drizzle one tablespoon olive oil over vegetables. Mix to coat. Roast in oven for 15-20 minutes.

2.   Put roasted vegetables in blender. Add all remaining ingredients into blender. Turn on low and slowly increase speed to high. Blend for 5-6 minutes until creamy.

CREAMY POTATO-LEEK SOUP

This is a thick, creamy soup. Serve with crusty bread for a complete meal.

Servings: 4

6 medium potatoes, peeled and cubed

1 tablespoon olive oil

2 leeks, washed, chopped

2 stalks celery, chopped

2 cup chicken broth

1 ½ cups heavy cream

1 teaspoon dried thyme

Sea salt and freshly ground black pepper, to taste

1.   Place potatoes in large pot, cover with water, bring to boil, reduce heat and simmer for 20 minutes or until potatoes are tender.

2.   In a medium skillet, heat olive oil over medium-high heat. Add leeks and celery and sauté for 7-8 minutes or until leeks are tender.

3.   Add potatoes, leek mixture, chicken broth, heavy creamy, thyme, salt, and pepper to blender. Turn blender on low and slowly increase speed to high. Blend for 30-40 seconds.

4.   Serve garnished with croutons.

AFRICAN SWEET POTATO AND PEANUT SOUP

This flavorful soup combines the tastes of sweet potatoes, peanuts, cilantro, and tomatoes into a fabulous combination.

Servings: 6

1 tablespoon olive oil

1 large yellow onion, chopped

3 cloves garlic, minced

2 teaspoons fresh ginger, minced

1 ½ teaspoons ground cumin

1 ½ teaspoons ground coriander

½ teaspoon cinnamon

¼ teaspoon ground cloves

1 (16 ounce) can chopped tomatoes

3 large sweet potatoes, peeled and cubed

1 large carrot, sliced

4 cups chicken broth

¼ teaspoon cayenne pepper

2 tablespoons peanut butter

¼ cup roasted peanuts, unsalted, chopped

1 bunch fresh cilantro chopped

1.　　In a large saucepan, heat olive oil over medium-high heat. Add onion and sauté for 5-6 minutes until soft. Add garlic, cumin, coriander, cinnamon, and cloves. Sauté for another minute. Add tomatoes, sweet potatoes, carrot, and chicken broth. Bring to boil, reduce heat and simmer, covered for 30 minutes.

2.　　Pour soup into blender. Add cayenne pepper and peanut butter. Turn blender on low and slowly increase speed to high. Blend for 30-40 seconds.

3.　　Serve topped chopped peanuts and cilantro.

FRESH TOMATO SOUP

··

Ripe tomatoes make this simple soup a standout.

Servings: 6

··

1 tablespoon olive oil

1 medium onion, chopped

3 cloves garlic

5 cups fresh tomatoes, chopped

3 cups chicken broth

3 tablespoons fresh basil or 1 teaspoon dried basil

2 tablespoons balsamic vinegar

1/2 teaspoon cayenne pepper

1 teaspoon thyme

1/2 cup heavy cream

½ teaspoon sugar

Salt and freshly ground black pepper, to taste

··

1.   Heat olive oil in pot over medium heat. Add onions and garlic and sauté for 3-4 minutes. Add tomatoes and chicken broth, bring to a boil, reduce heat and simmer for 15 minutes.

2.   Add tomato mixture to blender. Add in basil, vinegar, cayenne pepper, thyme, cream, sugar, salt, and pepper. Turn on low and slowly increase speed to high. Blend for 5-6 minutes until creamy.

3.   Adjust seasoning to taste before serving.

CREAM OF BROCCOLI SOUP

Cauliflower and almond milk give this soup its creamy texture.

Servings: 4

1 tablespoon extra-virgin olive oil

1 medium yellow onion, chopped

3 garlic cloves, minced

1 small head cauliflower, chopped into florets

2 cups almond milk, unsweetened

2 cups chicken broth

3 cups broccoli florets, chopped

Salt and freshly ground black pepper, to taste

1.   Heat olive oil in large saucepan over medium-high heat. Add onions and garlic and sauté for 2-3 minutes until onion turns translucent.

2.   Add cauliflower, almond milk, chicken broth, and broccoli. Cover pot and bring to boil. Reduce heat and simmer, covered, for 10 minutes or until cauliflower and broccoli florets are soft.

3.   Pour mixture into blender. Turn on low and slowly increase speed to high. Blend for 5-6 minutes until smooth.

4.   Season with salt and pepper before serving.

GAZPACHO

....

This garden-fresh soup is a cool treat on a summer day.

Servings: 4

....

2 plum tomatoes, chopped

½ cucumber, chopped

½ green bell pepper, chopped

½ red bell pepper, chopped

½ red onion, chopped

1 clove garlic, minced

2 cups tomato juice

½ teaspoon dried oregano

½ teaspoon dried basil

½ teaspoon salt

¼ teaspoon black pepper

1 ½ teaspoons Worcestershire sauce

1 teaspoon lemon juice

2 teaspoons red wine vinegar

....

1.   Put tomatoes, cucumber, bell pepper, onion, and garlic into blender. Blend on high for about 30 seconds. Add remaining ingredients. Pulse a few times to mix.

2.   Pour into container and chill in refrigerator for at least an hour before serving.

CURRIED CARROT SOUP

Lightly spiced, this soup is sure to please.

Servings: 6

2 tablespoons olive oil
1 yellow onion, chopped
2 cloves garlic, chopped
2 tablespoons curry powder
1 tablespoon cumin
2 pounds carrots, chopped
5 cups chicken broth
Sea salt and freshly ground black pepper, to taste
Yogurt or sour cream for garnish (optional)

1.   Heat oil in pot over medium heat. Add onion and garlic and sauté for 3-4 minutes until soft. Add curry powder, cumin, and carrots. Stir to coat carrots . Add broth, bring to boil, then reduce heat and summer for 15-20 minutes until carrots are tender.

2.   Transfer to blender. Season with salt and pepper. Turn blender on low and slowly increase speed to high. Blend for 30-40 seconds.

3.   Serve garnished with spoonful of yogurt or sour cream.

TUSCAN WHITE BEAN SOUP

This classic Italian soup is hearty enough to be a main course.

Servings: 6

4 slices bacon, chopped

1 medium yellow onion, chopped

1 stalk celery, chopped

1 carrot, chopped

3 cloves garlic, minced

3 (16 ounce) cans cannellini beans, rinsed and drained

1 bay leaf

1/2 cup white wine

4 cups chicken broth

1/4 teaspoon crushed red pepper flakes

1/4 cup fresh basil

Salt and freshly ground black pepper, to taste

1. Heat saucepan over medium-high heat. Add bacon, onion, celery, carrot, and garlic. Cook, stirring occasionally, for 4-5 minutes. Add beans, bay leaf, wine, broth, red pepper flakes, and basil. Reduce heat, cover, and cook for 20 minutes, until vegetables are tender.

2. Add soup to blender. Turn blender on low and slowly increase speed to high. Blend for 30-40 seconds.

FRESH ASPARAGUS SOUP

....

This soup is very easy to make and comes out creamy and delicious.

Servings: 4

....

1 pound fresh asparagus, bottoms trimmed

1 medium onion, chopped

2 cups chicken or vegetable broth, divided

1 tablespoon butter

2 tablespoons all-purpose flour

1/2 teaspoon salt

1/2 teaspoon freshly ground black pepper

1 cup milk

1/2 cup plain yogurt

Juice of 1/2 lemon

1/4 cup grated Parmesan cheese

....

1. Put asparagus and onion in sauce pan. Pour in 1/2 cup of broth. Bring to boil, reduce heat, and simmer for about 10 minutes until vegetables are tender. Pour mixture, including broth, into blender. Reserve a few asparagus stalks for garnish, if desired.

2. In the same pan, melt butter over low heat. Stir in flour, salt, and pepper. Cook for two minutes. Pour in remaining broth, increase heat and bring to boil. Remove from heat and pour into blender.

3. Add milk, yogurt and lemon juice to blender. Turn blender on low and slowly increase speed to high. Blend for 30-40 seconds.

4. Serve sprinkled with Parmesan cheese.

CURRIED PARSNIP AND PEAR SOUP

The blending of parsnips and pears, with the spice of curry, makes for a unique and flavorful soup.

Servings: 4

1 tablespoon olive oil
1 tablespoon butter
1 medium onion, chopped
1 tablespoon curry powder
1 teaspoon ground ginger
3 parsnips, peeled and sliced
2 large pears - peeled, cored, and chopped
4 cups chicken stock
1/2 cup coconut milk
Salt and freshly ground black pepper, to taste
1 pear, sliced, for garnish
Yogurt for serving (optional)

1.   Heat olive oil and butter in a saucepan over medium heat. Add onion, curry powder, and ginger and sauté until onion softens, about 5 minutes.

2.   Add parsnips and pears and stir to coat. Add chicken stock, bring to boil, reduce heat and simmer for 15-20 minutes until parsnips are soft.

3.   Pour mixture into blender. Add coconut milk, salt, and pepper. Turn blender on low and slowly increase speed to high. Blend for 30-40 seconds.

4.   Serve garnished with slice of pear and spoonful of yogurt.

4

Delicious Dips and Dressings

BABA GHANOUSH

This Middle Eastern dip is made with roasted eggplant. Makes a wonderful dip for pita bread or fresh vegetables.

Servings: 6

1 large eggplant
1/4 cup tahini
Juice of 1 lemon
2 cloves garlic, minced
2 tablespoons sesame seeds
Sea salt and freshly ground black pepper, to taste
1 tablespoon olive oil

1.   Preheat oven to 400 degrees F. Lightly grease a baking sheet.
2.   Pierce eggplant with fork a few times. Wrap in foil and place in oven. Roast it for 30 to 40 minutes, or until soft. Remove from oven, remove foil, and peel and discard skin.
3.   Place eggplant, tahini, lemon juice, sesame seeds, and garlic in blender. Season with salt and pepper to taste. Turn blender on low and slowly increase speed to high. Blend for 30-40 seconds.
4.   Transfer dip to serving bowl. Slowly mix in olive oil.
5.   Refrigerate for 2-3 hours before serving.

WHITE BEAN DIP

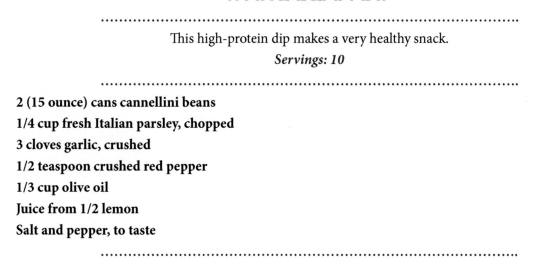

This high-protein dip makes a very healthy snack.

Servings: 10

2 (15 ounce) cans cannellini beans
1/4 cup fresh Italian parsley, chopped
3 cloves garlic, crushed
1/2 teaspoon crushed red pepper
1/3 cup olive oil
Juice from 1/2 lemon
Salt and pepper, to taste

1.   Place all ingredients in blender. Start on low and slowly increase speed to high. Blend for 1 minute.

ARTICHOKE-SPINACH DIP

....

Servings: 3 cups

....

2 cups fresh spinach

1 (14 ounce) can artichokes, drained

3 cloves garlic, crushed

1/2 cup plain Greek yogurt

2 (8 ounce) packages cream cheese, softened

2 tablespoons lemon juice

3/4 cup Parmesan cheese, grated

....

1.   Preheat oven to 365 degrees F.

2.   Place all ingredients in blender. Start on low and slowly increase speed to high. Blend for 1 minute.

3.   Spread mixture into lightly greased 7 x 11 baking dish.

4.   Bake, covered for 20 minutes. Remove cover and bake for an additional 5 minutes, until lightly browned.

HUMMUS

This healthy dip can be used as a spread on sandwiches or as a dip.

Servings: 8

1 (15ounce) can chickpeas, reserve liquid

2 cloves garlic, minced

1 1/2 tablespoons tahini

3/4 teaspoon ground cumin

2 tablespoons light sour cream

1/2 teaspoon salt

2 tablespoons lemon juice

1/4 teaspoon paprika

1.   Place all ingredients in blender. Start on low and slowly increase speed to high. Blend for 1 minute or until desired consistency is reached.

OLIVE TAPENADE

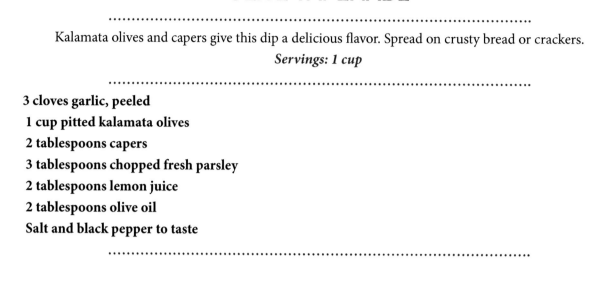

Kalamata olives and capers give this dip a delicious flavor. Spread on crusty bread or crackers.

Servings: 1 cup

3 cloves garlic, peeled

1 cup pitted kalamata olives

2 tablespoons capers

3 tablespoons chopped fresh parsley

2 tablespoons lemon juice

2 tablespoons olive oil

Salt and black pepper to taste

1.   Place all ingredients in blender. Start on low and slowly increase speed to high. Blend for 1 minute or until desired consistency is reached.

BLACK BEAN HUMMUS

Quick and easy, this tastes great as a sandwich with thick-cut tomatoes and crisp romaine lettuce.

Servings: 1 1/2 cups

1 (15 ounce) can black beans, rinsed and drained

2 cloves garlic, crushed

2 teaspoons lemon juice

1 tablespoon dried basil

1 teaspoon sesame oil

1/4 teaspoon cayenne pepper

1/4 teaspoon paprika

1.   Place all ingredients in blender. Start on low and slowly increase speed to high. Blend for 1 minute or until desired consistency is reached.

HOT CRAB DIP

Warm and creamy, this dip is great for entertaining.

Servings: 12

1 package (8 ounces) cream cheese, softened

1 small onion, finely chopped

3/4 cup mayonnaise

2 (6 ounce) cans crabmeat, drained

1 tablespoon lemon juice

1/8 teaspoon garlic powder

1/2 teaspoon cayenne pepper

3 tablespoons horseradish sauce

Sea salt and freshly ground black pepper, to taste

1/4 cup shredded cheddar cheese

1. Preheat oven to 350 degrees F.

2. Put all ingredients except for cheddar cheese in blender. Start on low and slowly increase speed to high. Blend for 1 minute or until desired consistency is reached.

3. Spread mixture evenly into 7 x 11 baking dish. Bake for 20 minutes covered. Uncover, sprinkle with cheese and bake or an additional 10 minutes, or until cheese is bubbly and golden brown.

GUACAMOLE

··

This is a smooth and creamy guacamole that makes the perfect dip for tortilla chips.

Servings: 4

··

2 Haas avocados, peeled, pitted and diced

2 Roma tomatoes, diced

4 tablespoons finely diced onion

3 cloves garlic, minced

1 tablespoon chopped cilantro

Juice of 1/2 lemon or lime

1/2 teaspoon sea salt, or to taste

··

1.   Place all ingredients in blender. Start on low and slowly increase speed to high. Blend for 1 minute or until desired consistency is reached.

RED PEPPER HUMMUS

Change up your traditional hummus with this red pepper variation.

Servings: 8

....

1 (16 ounce) can chick peas, drained and rinsed

1 tablespoon extra-virgin olive oil

1 medium red bell pepper, chopped

2 cloves garlic, crushed

1 tablespoon tahini

Juice of 1 lemon

1 teaspoon ground cumin

1/2 teaspoon cayenne pepper

1/4 cup fresh basil

1/2 teaspoon salt

1/4 teaspoon ground black pepper

....

1.   Place all ingredients in blender. Start on low and slowly increase speed to high. Blend for 1 minute or until desired consistency is reached.

SPINACH DIP

This is a flavorful spinach dip. Serve in a bread bowl with crudités.

Servings: 8

1 cup mayonnaise

1 (16 ounce) container sour cream

2 garlic cloves, crushed

1/2 cup onion, diced

1 (4 ounce) can water chestnuts, drained and chopped

1 (10 ounce) package frozen chopped spinach, thawed and drained

1 (1 pound) loaf round sourdough bread

1.   Place all ingredients except for bread in blender. Start on low and slowly increase speed to high. Blend for 1 minute or until desired consistency is reached.

2.   Chill in refrigerator for at least an hour and up to overnight.

3.   When ready to serve: Preheat oven to 350 degrees F. Cut top off of sourdough bread and remove interior. Place on baking sheet and heat in oven for 10 minutes.

4.   Remove bread from oven and fill with spinach dip mixture and serve.

TZATZIKI

....

This traditional Greek dip gets better as it sits so make it the day before if you can.

Servings: 5 cups

....

1 (32 ounce) container plain Greek style yogurt

1 English cucumber with peel, diced, divided in half

1 clove garlic, pressed

2 tablespoons fresh lime juice

2 tablespoons extra-virgin olive oil

2 teaspoons grated lemon zest

3 tablespoons chopped fresh dill

1 teaspoon salt

1 teaspoon fresh ground black pepper

....

1.   Place yogurt, 1/2 of cucumber, garlic, lemon juice, olive oil, lemon zest, dill, salt, and pepper in blender. Pulse on and off, on speed 8, several times. Should still be a little chunky. Check consistency and pulse a few more times if needed.

2.   Pour into serving dish, top with remaining chopped cucumber, cover and refrigerate for at least a couple of hours and preferably overnight.

LEMON-DILL YOGURT DRESSING

A tangy dip, try it in place of mayonnaise on potato salad.
Servings: Makes 1 cup

1 cup plain Greek yogurt
1 tablespoon fresh lemon juice
1 teaspoon grated lemon zest
1/4 cup extra-virgin olive oil
1/4 teaspoon ground black pepper
2 teaspoons fresh dill, chopped

1.   Place all ingredients in blender. Start on low and slowly increase speed to high. Blend for 30 seconds or until desired consistency is reached.

2.   Chill in refrigerator for at least an hour before serving.

RASPBERRY WINE VINAIGRETTE

Servings: Makes 1 1/2 cups

1/2 cup extra-virgin olive oil

1/2 cup raspberry wine vinegar

1/3 cup white sugar

2 teaspoons Dijon mustard

1/2 teaspoon dried oregano

1/2 teaspoon ground black pepper

1. Place all ingredients in blender. Pulse on and off, on speed 8, several times.
2. Store in glass container in refrigerator.

GARLICKY RANCH DRESSING

This works equally well as a dip, salad dressing, or topping on baked potatoes.

Servings: Makes 2 cups

1 cup buttermilk

2/3 cup mayonnaise

2/3 cup sour cream

2 cloves garlic, crushed

1 teaspoon onion powder

2 teaspoons chopped fresh chives

2 teaspoons chopped fresh dill

2 teaspoons chopped fresh parsley

1 teaspoon salt

1/4 teaspoon pepper

1. Place all ingredients in blender. Start on low and slowly increase speed to high. Blend for 30 seconds or until desired consistency is reached.

2. Chill in refrigerator for at least an hour before serving.

SALSA

....

This salsa makes a great quick, easy, and healthy snack. Whips up in minutes.

Servings: 8

....

1 (4 ounce) can of green chilies with liquid

1 tablespoon fresh lemon juice

1/4 red onion, chopped

2 cloves garlic, crushed

1/2 teaspoon sea salt

1/2 teaspoon ground cumin

1/4 teaspoon cayenne pepper

1 (14.5 ounce) can of diced tomatoes

1/4 cup fresh cilantro leaves

....

1.   Place all ingredients in blender. Pulse on and off, on speed 8, several times. Should still be a little chunky. Check consistency and pulse a few more times if needed.

5

Sensational Sauces

BASIL PESTO

....

This is the classic version of pesto sauce. Good on pasta, pizza, spread on bread, and more.

Servings: Makes 2 cups

....

1/4 cup pine nuts

3 cups packed fresh basil leaves

4 cloves garlic

3/4 cup grated Parmesan cheese

1/2 cup olive oil

....

1.   Preheat oven to 350 degrees F. Spread pine nut in single layer on baking sheet. Bake for about 10 minutes, or until light golden brown. Be sure to keep an eye on them, because they can get overly browned very quickly.

2.   Place toasted pine nuts, basil, garlic, Parmesan cheese, and olive oil into blender. Start on low and slowly increase speed to high. Blend for 30 seconds or until desired consistency is reached.

CHIMICHURRI SAUCE

This sauce is of Argentinian origin and is popular on grilled meats.

Servings: Makes 1 1/2 cups

1 1/2 cups fresh parsley

3 cloves garlic, crushed

3/4 cup extra virgin olive oil

3 tablespoons red wine vinegar

2 tablespoons dried oregano

2 teaspoons ground cumin

1/2 teaspoon salt

1/2 tablespoon hot sauce

1.   Place all ingredients in blender. Start on low and slowly increase speed to high. Blend for 30 seconds or until desired consistency is reached.

HOLLANDAISE SAUCE

....

This is the easiest way to make this classic sauce.

Servings: 6

....

3 egg yolks

1/4 teaspoon Dijon mustard

1 tablespoon lemon juice

1 dash hot pepper sauce , such as Tabasco sauce

1/2 cup butter, melted

....

1.   In blender, combine the egg yolks, mustard, lemon juice and hot pepper sauce. Cover, and blend on high for 30 seconds.

2.   Reduce speed and slowly pour the butter into the egg yolk mixture in a thin stream. Blend for another 15 seconds or until desired consistency.

MARINARA SAUCE

....

Making your own marinara sauce is really simple and much healthier than jarred sauce.

Servings: 4 cups

....

6 tablespoons olive oil

 1/3 cup finely diced onion

2 (14.5 ounce) cans stewed tomatoes

 1 (6 ounce) can tomato paste

 4 tablespoons chopped fresh parsley

 1 clove garlic, minced

 1 teaspoon dried oregano

 1 teaspoon salt

 1/4 teaspoon ground black pepper

 1/2 cup white wine

....

1.   Heat olive oil in a large skillet over medium heat. Add onion and sauté for 2 minutes. Add to blender with remaining ingredients. Start on low and slowly increase speed to high. Blend for 30 seconds or until desired consistency is reached.

2.   Pour sauce in saucepan and simmer over low heat for 30 minutes.

PESTO ROSSO

This red pesto is made using sun-dried tomatoes. It can be used as a sauce for pasta, brushed on grilled meats, or spread on crusty bread for a simple bruschetta.

Servings: Makes 1 1/2 cups

1 cup extra-virgin olive oil

½ cup toasted blanched almonds, chopped

2 tablespoons rosemary leaves, minced

2 teaspoons balsamic vinegar

2 teaspoons sugar

½ teaspoon paprika

20 pitted black olives

10 sun-dried tomatoes in oil, chopped

4 cloves garlic, chopped

Sea salt and freshly ground black pepper, to taste

1.   Place all ingredients into blender. Start on low and slowly increase speed to high. Blend for 30 seconds or until desired consistency is reached.

ARTICHOKE PESTO

1 (12 ounce) jar artichokes, with liquid

1/4 cup chopped fresh basil

4 medium garlic cloves

Juice of 2 lemons

1/2 teaspoon cayenne pepper

1 cup walnuts

1/2 cup olive oil

Sea salt and ground pepper, to taste

1/2 cup grated Parmesan cheese

1.   Place all ingredients in blender. Start on low and slowly increase speed to high. Blend for 30 seconds. Check consistency and blend more as needed. Can be left slightly chunky or blended smooth.

ALFREDO SAUCE

This rich and creamy sauce makes a perfect accompaniment to fettuccine. Toss in roasted chicken or grilled shrimp and lightly steamed broccoli for a delicious meal.

Servings: 4

1/4 cup butter, melted

1 cup heavy cream

2 cloves garlic, crushed

1 1/2 cups freshly grated Parmesan cheese

1/4 cup chopped fresh parsley

1/2 teaspoon nutmeg

Salt and freshly ground black pepper, to taste

1.   Place all ingredients in blender. Start on low and slowly increase speed to high. Blend for 5 minutes.

BARBECUE SAUCE

....

Servings: 2 cups

....

2 cups chopped tomatoes

1/4 cup apple cider vingear

3 tablespoons soy sauce

1 1/2 tablespoons brown mustard

1 tablespoon hot sauce

1 tablespoon lemon juice

1 tablespoon liquid smoke

1 teaspoon sea salt

1 teaspoon garlic powder

1 teaspoon onion powder

1 teaspoon molasses

....

1.   Place all ingredients in blender. Start on low and slowly increase speed to high. Blend for 5 minutes.

6

Superfood Smoothies

AVOCADO SMOOTHIE

Smooth, creamy, and delicious.

Servings: 4 cups

1 ripe avocado, halved and pitted

1 banana

1 cup almond milk

1/2 cup vanilla yogurt

3 tablespoons honey

8 ice cubes

1.   Place all ingredients into blender. Start on low and slowly increase speed to high. Blend for 45 seconds or until desired consistency is reached.

PINEAPPLE COCONUT BANANA SMOOTHIE

....

This healthy pina colada inspired smoothie tastes so good.

Servings: 1

....

4 ice cubes

1/4 cup fresh pineapple cubes (can substitute canned or frozen)

1 large banana, cut into chunks

½ cup coconut milk

3/4 cup pineapple or apple juice

....

1.   Place all ingredients into blender. Start on low and slowly increase speed to high. Blend for 45 seconds or until desired consistency is reached.

ORANGE PAPAYA CARROT SMOOTHIE

Servings: 2

1 banana

1 /2 cup papaya cubes (about 1 papaya)

½ cup fresh pineapple cubes

1 large carrot, sliced

½ cup seedless grapes (optional)

3 ice cubes

1 (6 ounce) container plain yogurt

½ cup orange juice

1.   Place all ingredients into blender. Start on low and slowly increase speed to high. Blend for 45 seconds or until desired consistency is reached.

MOCHA SMOOTHIE

....

Coffee gives this smoothie an energizing kick.

Servings: 1

....

1 cup ice

3/4 cup coconut milk

1/4 cup brewed coffee

1 tablespoon sugar or honey

1 tablespoon cacao powder or nibs

1 tablespoon vanilla extract

....

1.   Place all ingredients into blender. Start on low and slowly increase speed to high. Blend for 45 seconds or until desired consistency is reached.

APPLE BEET DETOX SMOOTHIE

....

Servings: 2

....

2 beets, peeled and cut into chunks

1 apple, cored and sliced

1 pear, cored and sliced

½ cup frozen berries (optional)

1 cup ice cubes

¾ cup apple juice

....

1.　　Place all ingredients into blender. Start on low and slowly increase speed to high. Blend for 45 seconds or until desired consistency is reached.

CHERRY SMOOTHIE

Try this refreshing smoothie on a hot summer day for an invigorating treat.

Servings: 2

2 cups cherries, pitted

1 cup mango, chopped (fresh or frozen)

½ cup plain yogurt

¾ cup coconut milk

½ cup ice cubes

1.   Place all ingredients into blender. Start on low and slowly increase speed to high. Blend for 45 seconds or until desired consistency is reached.

GINGER-ORANGE SMOOTHIE

....

Ginger has many health benefits including being very beneficial for digestion.

Servings: 2

....

1 carrot, sliced

1 cup pineapple chunks

1 tablespoon fresh ginger, minced

1 cup orange juice

....

1.   Place all ingredients into blender. Start on low and slowly increase speed to high. Blend for 45 seconds or until desired consistency is reached.

PEANUT BUTTER BANANA SMOOTHIE

Simple and delicious, this is a kid (and grownup) favorite.

Servings 4

2 bananas

2 cups milk (can substitute with nut milk of choice)

½ cup peanut butter

½ cup oats

2 tablespoons honey

1 teaspoon vanilla

2 cups ice cubes

1.   Place all ingredients into blender. Start on low and slowly increase speed to high. Blend for 45 seconds or until desired consistency is reached.

MANGO GINGER SMOOTHIE

....

Servings: 2

....

1/4 cup orange juice

1 mango, sliced

1 frozen banana, sliced

2 baby carrots

1 (6 ounce) container vanilla yogurt

2 ice cubes

1 tablespoon fresh ginger, minced

....

1.   Place all ingredients into blender. Start on low and slowly increase speed to high. Blend for 45 seconds or until desired consistency is reached.

ALMOND-BLUEBERRY SMOOTHIE

This smoothie is an antioxidant powerhouse. Try it when you need a boost.

Servings: 2

1 cup almond milk

1 cup blueberries, fresh or frozen

4 ice cubes (less if using frozen blueberries)

1 teaspoon vanilla extract

1 tablespoon almond butter

1 tablespoon chia seeds

1.   Place all ingredients into blender. Start on low and slowly increase speed to high. Blend for 45 seconds or until desired consistency is reached.

CHOCOLATE MILKSHAKE

....

Bananas give this milkshake a creamy taste.

Servings: 2

....

2 bananas

¾ cup milk

2 tablespoons cocoa powder

1 teaspoon vanilla extract

1 tablespoon honey (optional)

Pinch of sea salt

1 cup ice cubes

....

1.   Place all ingredients into blender. Start on low and slowly increase speed to high. Blend for 45 seconds or until desired consistency is reached.

Variation: Change this to a Strawberry Milkshake by substituting 1 cup sliced strawberries for the cocoa powder.

7

Frozen Concoctions

FROZEN STRAWBERRY MARGARITA

....

Make up a batch of this delicious margarita at your next party.

Servings: 4

....

6 ounces tequila

2 ounces triple sec

1 cup frozen sliced strawberries in syrup

4 ounces frozen limeade concentrate

....

1.   Place all ingredients into blender. Start on low and slowly increase speed to high. Blend for 45 seconds or until desired consistency is reached.

2.   Serve in margarita glasses rimmed in sugar.

LEMON SORBET

Icy and delicious, this tart sorbet is fantastic on a hot day.

Servings: 2

1 lemon, peeled

¼ cup sugar

3 ½ cups ice

1.   Place all ingredients in blender. Start on low and slowly increase speed to high. Blend for 45 seconds or until desired consistency is reached.

2.   Serve immediately.

TRIPLE BERRY SORBET

Very refreshing!

Servings: 4

2 cups frozen strawberries

1 cup frozen raspberries

1 cup frozen blackberries

1 cup sugar

2 cups ice

¾ cup water

1/2 cup lime juice

2 tablespoons frozen orange juice concentrate

1. Place all ingredients in blender. Start on low and slowly increase speed to high. Blend for 45 seconds or until desired consistency is reached.

2. Serve immediately.

Strawberry Granita

A granite is a type of Italian ice, similar to a snow cone.

Servings: 8

2 pounds ripe strawberries

1/3 cup white sugar, or to taste

1 cup water

1/2 teaspoon lemon juice

1/4 teaspoon balsamic vinegar

Pinch of sea salt

1.   Place all ingredients in blender. Start on low and slowly increase speed to high. Blend for 45 seconds.

2.   Transfer mixture to baking dish and put in freezer. Every 30-45 minutes stir with fork, moving crystals from edges to center. Repeat this process 3-4 times or until the granite is light and fluffy, similar to a snow cone consistency.

PUREED RAINBOW FRUIT POPS

Kids just love these colorful pops. If you don't have popsicle molds you can make them in small paper or plastic cups with wooden craft sticks.

Servings: 6

3/4 cup kiwi chunk, fresh or frozen

3/4 cup mango chunks, fresh or frozen

¾ cup raspberries, fresh or frozen

3 tablespoon sugar, or to taste

12 tablespoons water

1.   Each fruit will need to be pureed separately in the blender. Add one type of fruit, 1 tablespoon sugar, and 4 tablespoons of water to blender. Start on low and slowly increase speed to high. Blend for about 45 seconds. Pour into bowl. Repeat process for each type of fruit.

2.   Pour a layer of raspberry puree into each popsicle mold or cup. Place in freezer for about an hour.

3.   Add mango layer and return to freezer for about 45 minutes. Remove from freezer and insert wooden stick(s).

4.   Return to freezer and freeze until layer is solid, about 2 hours.

5.   Add layer of kiwi puree. Return to freezer until solid.

PINA COLADA

This tastes like being on a tropical vacation.

Servings: 4

···

3 cups ice

1 cup diced pineapple, frozen

4 ounces pineapple juice

2 ounces coconut cream

3 ounces white rum

2 ounce dark rum

Pineapple slices for garnish

···

1.   Place all ingredients into blender. Start on low and slowly increase speed to high. Blend for 45 seconds or until desired consistency is reached.

2.   Serve garnished with pineapple slices

8

... And More

CRUNCHY COLESLAW

....

Servings: 8

....

1 medium head cabbage

1 carrot

1 cucumber, peeled

1/4 onion, chopped

1 clove garlic, crushed

1/4 cup extra-virgin olive oil

1/4 cup red wine vinegar

3 tablespoons cup white sugar (optional)

Sea salt and freshly ground black pepper, to taste

....

1.   Chop each vegetable (cabbage, carrot, cucumber) separately in blender. Pulse several times on high to achieve desired texture. Combine in large bowl.

2.   Make dressing by putting onion, garlic, olive oil, vinegar, sugar, salt, and pepper into blender. Blend for about 45 seconds. Pour over shredded vegetables and toss well to combine.

HOMEMADE APPLESAUCE

··

This is simple and much better than jarred applesauce.

Servings: 4

··

4 apples, peeled, cored, chopped

¾ cup water

1/2 teaspoon cinnamon

¼ cup brown sugar

··

1.   Place apples into saucepan and add about an inch of water. Bring to boil, reduce heat, cover and simmer for about 5 minutes or until apples are tender.

2.   Add apples along with remaining ingredients to blender. Blend, starting on low and then increasing to high for about 30 seconds or until desired consistency.

PIZZA DOUGH

Didn't know you could make pizza in your Ninja Blender? Well, it's true and very easy, too.

Servings: Makes 2 12-inch thin crusts

2 1/2 cups all-purpose flour

1 envelope yeast

3/4 teaspoon salt

2 tablespoons olive oil

1 cup very warm water (120 degrees F to 130 degrees F)

1.   Add flour, yeast, and salt to blender. Pulse a couple of time to combine. Add olive oil and pulse to combine.

2.   Add water, ¼ cup at a time, pulsing a few times with each addition. Continue until dough is formed. Do not over blend.

3.   Lightly flour work surface, add dough, and knead until smooth and elastic.

4.   Place ball of dough into bowl, cover with dish towel, and let rest for about 15 minutes.

5.   Divide and roll dough to desired thickness. Place on lightly oiled pizza pans.

6.   Add toppings and bake at 400 degrees F for 20 to 30 minutes.

BREADCRUMBS

....

This is a great use of bread that has become too hard to eat. Don't throw it away, make breadcrumbs instead.

Servings: About 3 cups (depending on size of bread you are using)

....

Bread, leftover, stale bread

....

1. Preheat oven to 300 degrees F.
2. Cut bread into pieces. Place in blender and pulse to blend until you have the desired consistency for your breadcrumbs.
3. Spread breadcrumbs in thin layer on baking sheet.
4. Bake in oven, stirring occasionally to toast all sides, until lightly browned, about 15 minutes.
5. Cool completely before storing in airtight container.

Tip: For seasoned breadcrumbs, add seasonings of choice to blender before blending. Try oregano, rosemary, or basil.

WHIPPED CREAM

Homemade real whipped cream simply cannot be beat.

Servings: 2 cups

2 cups whipping cream

2 tablespoons sugar, or to taste

1 teaspoon vanilla extract

1. Place all ingredients in blender. Blend, starting on low and then increasing to high for about 15-20 seconds or until soft peaks form.
2. Store in refrigerator until ready to serve.

CAULI-RICE

Making "rice" from cauliflower is very popular with people following low-carb or Paleo diets. Using your Vitamix for the task makes it simple.

Servings: About 2 cups

1 head cauliflower

1. Wash cauliflower and break into florets,
2. Place in blender and blend on low until cauliflower resembles grains of rice.
3. Store in freezer bags until ready to use.

SWEET POTATO BREAD

Servings: Makes 1 loaf

1 large sweet potato, peeled and cubed

1 cup white sugar

1/2 cup canola oil

2 eggs

1 3/4 cups all-purpose flour

1 teaspoon baking soda

1/4 teaspoon salt

1/2 teaspoon ground cinnamon

1/2 teaspoon ground nutmeg

1/3 cup water

1/2 cup chopped pecans

1. Preheat oven to 350 degrees F.

2. Place sweet potato cubes into saucepan. Add water just cover potatoes. Bring to boil, reduce heat, and simmer until tender, about 15 minutes.

3. Add sweet potatoes to blender along with all ingredients except for pecans. Blend, starting on low and increasing to high for about 30 seconds or until well blended.

4. Pour batter into lightly greased 9 x 5 loaf pan. Sprinkle with pecans. Bake for one hour or until toothpick inserted in center comes out clean.

BANANA OAT PANCAKES

2 cups rolled oats

2 bananas

2 eggs

1/2 cup whole wheat flour

1 ¼ cups almond milk

1 tablespoon baking powder

1 tablespoon vanilla

½ teaspoon cinnamon

Pinch of salt

1.   Add all ingredients to blender. Blend on medium speed for 30 seconds or until batter is smooth.

2.   Cook on greased, preheated skillet, flipping once, until golden brown on both sides.

MAYONNAISE

Servings: 1 cup

1 whole egg
2 tablespoons distilled vinegar
½ teaspoon salt
½ teaspoon dry mustard
¾ cup olive oil

1.   Put egg, vinegar, salt, and mustard into blender. Blend on high for about 10 seconds. Reduce speed to medium and slowly trickle in olive oil through top. Blend for another 30 seconds until thick.
2.   Store in refrigerator in airtight container. Will last about 3 weeks.

KETCHUP

Store bought ketchup is loaded with sugar, dyes, and fillers. Make your own for a health and flavor boost.

Servings: Makes 4 cups

28-oz. can tomato puree
1 medium yellow onion, peeled and quartered
2 cloves garlic, crushed
2 tablespoons brown sugar
1/2 cup cider vinegar
1 cup water
1 teaspoon dry mustard
½ teaspoon cayenne pepper
½ teaspoon ground allspice
½ teaspoon ground ginger
½ teaspoon ground cinnamon
½ teaspoon sea salt
½ teaspoon ground black pepper

1.   Add all ingredients to blender. Blend on high for 30 seconds or until smooth.
2.   Pour into large saucepan, bring to boil, reduce heat, and simmer for an hour, stirring occasionally.
3.   Pour into airtight containers and store in refrigerator for up to a month.

DIJON MUSTARD

Servings: Makes 1 cup

1/3 cup mustard seeds
1/3 cup cider vinegar
1/3 cup water
1 teaspoon brown sugar
1 teaspoon ground turmeric
1/2 teaspoon salt
½ teaspoon cayenne pepper

1.   Place all ingredients in blender. Blend on high for 60 seconds or until smooth.
2.   Store in airtight container in refrigerator for up to 4 months.

FROM THE AUTHOR

Thank you for reading the *Ninja Blender Cookbook: Fast Healthy Blender Recipes for Soups, Sauces, Smoothies, Dips, and More*. I sincerely hope that you found this book informative and helpful and that it helps you to create delicious foods for yourself, family, and friends.

Happy blending!

MORE BESTSELLING TITLES FROM DYLANNA PRESS

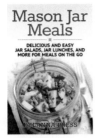

Mason Jar Meals by Dylanna Press

Mason jar meals are a fun and practical way to take your meals on the go. Mason jars are an easy way to prepare individual servings, so whether you're cooking for one, two, or a whole crowd, these fun, make-ahead meals will work.

Includes More than 50 Recipes and Full-Color Photos

In this book, you'll find a wide variety of recipes including all kinds of salads, as well as hot meal ideas such as mini chicken pot pies and lasagna in a jar. Also included are mouth-watering desserts such as strawberry shortcake, apple pie, and s'mores.

The recipes are easy to prepare and don't require any special cooking skills. So what are you waiting for? Grab your Mason jars and start preparing these gorgeous and tasty dishes!

The Inflammation Diet by Dylanna Press

Beat Pain, Slow Aging, and Reduce Risk of Heart Disease with the Inflammation Diet

Inflammation has been called the "silent killer" and it has been linked to a wide variety of illnesses including heart disease, arthritis, diabetes, chronic pain, autoimmune disorders, and cancer.

Often, the root of chronic inflammation is in the foods we eat.

The Inflammation Diet: Complete Guide to Beating Pain and Inflammation will show you how, by making simple changes to your diet, you can greatly reduce inflammation in your body and reduce your symptoms and lower your risk of chronic disease.

The book includes a complete plan for eliminating inflammation and implementing an anti-inflammatory diet:

- Overview of inflammation and the body's immune response – what can trigger it and why chronic inflammation is harmful
- The link between diet and inflammation
- Inflammatory foods to avoid
- Anti-inflammatory foods to add to your diet to beat pain and inflammation
- Over 50 delicious inflammation diet recipes
- A 14-day meal plan

Take charge of your health and implement the inflammation diet to lose weight, slow the aging process, eliminate chronic pain, and reduce the likelihood and symptoms of chronic disease.

Learn how to heal your body from within through diet.

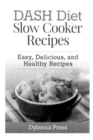

DASH Diet Slow Cooker Recipes by Dylanna Press
Delicious and Healthy DASH Diet Recipes for Your Slow Cooker
The DASH diet has once again been named the healthiest diet by top nutrition experts and there's no better time to start reaping the rewards of this smart, sensible eating plan. Eating the DASH diet way does not have to be boring, in fact, it contains the most delicious foods around – lean meats, whole grains, lots of fresh fruits and vegetables, and flavorful herbs and spices. So whether you are just starting out on the DASH diet or have been eating low-sodium for years, the DASH Diet Slow Cooker Recipes: Easy, Delicious, and Healthy Recipes is going to help you make delicious, healthy meals without spending a lot of time in the kitchen.
For this book, we've collected the best slow cooker recipes and adapted them to the DASH diet to create mouthwatering, family-pleasing dishes that can all be prepared easily and then cooked in your slow cooker while you're off doing other things. There's really nothing better than coming home at the end of a hectic day to the smell of tonight's dinner already prepared and waiting to be eaten.

These recipes feature fresh, whole foods and include a wide variety of recipes to appeal to every taste from classic dishes to new twists that just may become your new favorites. In addition, each recipe has less than 500 mg of sodium per serving, many a lot less than that.

In addition to recipes, the book includes a brief overview of the DASH diet as well as tips on how to get the most out of your slow cooker.

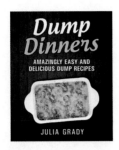

Dump Dinners: Amazingly Easy and Delicious Dump Recipes by Julia Grady

With the hectic pace of today's lifestyles getting dinner on the table every night is no easy task. When pressed for time, dump dinners make the perfect solution to the question, What's for dinner?

Dump dinners are so popular because they are so easy to make.

These recipes feature simple ingredients that you probably already have on hand in your freezer, refrigerator, and pantry. They do not require complicated cooking techniques or that you stand over the stove, stirring and sautéing. The majority of the recipes are mixed right in the pan they are cooked in, with the added bonus of saving cleanup time.

Delicious, Quick Recipes Your Family Will Love

This book contains the best dump dinner recipes around. None of these recipes take more than 15 minutes of hands-on time to prepare, and most a lot less. When you're short on time, you can turn to any one of these delicious recipes and have a home-cooked meal on the table with little effort and big rewards.

The recipes in this book can be cooked in several ways:

- Baked in the oven
- Cooked in a slow cooker
- Cooked on the stovetop
- Microwaved
- Frozen and cooked later

So whether you'd like to throw something in the slow cooker and come home hours later to an aromatic meal or pop a quickly prepared casserole into the oven, you are sure to find a recipe you and your family will love.

Index

Manufactured by Amazon.ca
Bolton, ON

22886402R00109